52 WEEKS

MINISTRY
OF THE
Husband

DEVOTIONAL

52 WEEKS MINISTRY OF THE HUSBAND DEVOTIONAL

Copyright © 2025 by Douglas Asante

All rights reserved. No portion of this book may be reproduced, stored in a retrieval system, or transmitted in any form or by any means - electronic, mechanical, photocopy, recording, scanning, or other - except for brief quotations in critical reviews or articles, without the prior written permission of the publisher.

ISBN: 978-1-916692-40-4

Email the author via **info@dasante.org.uk**
Visit the website for more information: **www.dasante.org.uk**

Published in the United Kingdom by
Equip Publishing House

DEDICATION

To my beloved wife, Diana, whose love and partnership continually inspire this ministry, and to every husband seeking to honour God in his calling.

— Douglas

ACKNOWLEDGEMENTS

I give glory to God, the Author and Sustainer of marriage.

Special thanks to my family for their support, patience, and encouragement throughout the writing of this devotional.

I am grateful also to the leaders, friends, and mentors who have prayed with me, shared wisdom, and walked alongside me in ministry.

This work is dedicated to every husband who desires to live faithfully as priest, prophet, and king in his home.

CONTENTS

Dedication iii
Acknowledgements iv
Introduction vii
How to Use This Book ix

Foundations of the Husband's Calling

Called to Lead 1
Honouring Your Wife 3
Loving as Christ Loves 5
Working in Unity With Your Wife 7
Fatherhood as Responsibility, Not Just Childbearing 9
Companionship in Marriage 11
Communication That Builds Connection 13
Faithfulness in All Things 15
The Husband as Priest of the Home 17
The Husband as Prophet of the Home 19
The Husband as King of the Home 21
Spiritual Covering and Protection 23

Building the Home in Strength and Grace

Financial Stewardship in Marriage 25
Building a Home on Prayer 27
Leading by Example 29
The Power of Humility in Marriage 31
The Husband as a Man of Integrity 33
Forgiveness in Marriage 35
Cultivating Patience in Marriage 37
Emotional Mastery in Marriage 39
The Husband as a Peacemaker 41
The Power of Faith in Family Life 43
The Husband as a Man of Prayer 45
Walking in the Word 47

The Husband as a Man of Wisdom 49
The Husband as Provider 51
The Husband as Protector 53
The Husband as Encourager 55
Restoring Trust After Failure 57

Growing in Maturity and Unity

The Husband as Servant Leader 59
The Husband as Visionary 61
The Husband as Builder of Legacy 63
Resolving Conflict God's Way 65
The Power of Agreement in Marriage 67
The Husband as Spiritual Leader 69
The Husband as Intercessor 71
The Husband as Shepherd of His Home 73
The Husband as Teacher of the Word 75
The Husband as Example of Faith 77
The Husband as Steward of Time 79
Creating a Culture of Peace at Home 81
The Husband as Anchor in Times of Storm 83
The Husband as Source of Joy 85
The Husband as Spiritual Warrior 87
The Husband as Vessel of Grace 89
The Husband as Example of Love 91
The Husband as Encourager of Faith 93
Guarding the Gates of Your Home 95
The Husband as Peacemaker and Mediator 97
The Husband as Source of Strength and Stability 99
The Husband as Instrument of Blessing 101
Living as a Lifelong Priest 103

Closing Reflection

Final Reflection 105
Prayer of Commitment 106
Final Journalling Prompts 106

INTRODUCTION

Marriage is one of God's greatest gifts and one of His most profound callings. It is not merely a social contract or a cultural tradition; it is a divine covenant designed to reflect God's nature and His relationship with His people. From the beginning, God declared, "It is not good that man should be alone" (Genesis 2:18). He created woman and brought her to the man, establishing marriage as a sacred union with eternal purpose.

At the heart of this covenant lies the husband's calling. A husband is not simply a provider or a bearer of the family name. He is called to be priest, prophet, and king in his home.

As **priest**, he leads his household into God's presence through prayer and spiritual covering.

As **prophet**, he declares God's truth and helps his family discern His will.

As **king**, he governs with wisdom, humility, and sacrificial love.

This ministry of husbandhood is central to God's design. When husbands neglect their role, homes lose direction and families struggle to reflect Christ's love. But when they rise to their calling, marriages flourish and Christ's light shines through the home.

This 52-week devotional is designed to guide husbands into that calling with clarity and consistency. Each week offers Scripture, reflection, prayer, and practical application — not to overwhelm but to transform.

You will be challenged to examine your heart, encouraged to love your wife with Christlike devotion, and equipped to lead your home with faith and grace. Husbandhood is not a title to claim — it is a ministry to be lived daily.

As you journey through these pages, remember: God has already equipped you for this task. His Word is your foundation, His Spirit your helper, and His grace your strength. May this devotional enrich your marriage, deepen your faith, and help you leave a legacy of love that endures.

HOW TO USE THIS BOOK

This devotional is a practical tool to help husbands grow in spiritual maturity and leadership over 52 weeks. It is designed for weekly reflection and daily application.

1 Establish a Weekly Rhythm

At the start of each week, read the Scripture aloud and meditate on it. Move through each section — Observation, Interpretation, Illustration, Correlation, Application, and Prayer — before journalling your reflections.

2 Engage Daily

Break each week into daily focus points:

- Day 1: Scripture & Observation
- Day 2: Interpretation
- Day 3: Illustration or Story
- Day 4: Correlation Scriptures
- Day 5: Application Step
- Day 6: Prayer (alone or with your wife/family)
- Day 7: Journalling & Reflection

3 Journal Faithfully

Use the prompts to record insights, prayers, and progress. Your journal will become a testimony of God's work in your life and home.

4 Apply Intentionally

Treat each Application as a spiritual assignment. Transformation, not information, is the goal.

5 Share with Others

Study alongside your wife, a men's fellowship, or a church group. Growth multiplies in community.

6 Revisit and Repeat

After 52 weeks, start again. Each season of life will bring new understanding.

7 Depend on the Holy Spirit

Pray for His guidance daily. Only through His grace can you fulfil your role as husband effectively.

W E E K 1

Called to Lead

"Then God said, 'Let Us make man in Our image, according to Our likeness; let them have dominion over the fish of the sea, over the birds of the air, over the cattle, over all the earth, and over every creeping thing that creeps on the earth.'"

GENESIS 1:26 (NKJV)

OBSERVATION

In the creation narrative, man is given a unique identity — made in God's image and likeness. Leadership is entrusted as stewardship, not domination.

INTERPRETATION

To be a husband is a divine calling. Leadership in the home is not about control or self-interest but about sacrificial service, accountability, and reflecting God's heart towards one's family.

ILLUSTRATION

Consider an orchestra without a conductor. Each musician may be skilled and each instrument finely tuned, yet without leadership the music lacks harmony. In the same way, a family may possess talent and potential, but without godly leadership it risks drifting without clear direction.

Correlation

- Matthew 20:27–28 — Leadership is service.
- 1 Corinthians 11:3 — The divine order of headship.
- Joshua 24:15 — A household serving the Lord.

Application

- Begin each day with prayer.
- Serve your wife and children in practical ways.
- Lead a short family devotion this week.
- Make at least one decision prayerfully, seeking God's wisdom before acting.

Prayer

Heavenly Father, thank You for entrusting me with the responsibility of leadership in my home. Teach me to lead with humility, wisdom, and love. May my actions reflect the heart of Christ, and may my leadership draw my family closer to You. Strengthen me to serve faithfully, to make decisions guided by Your Spirit, and to set an example that honours Your name. Amen.

Journalling Prompts

- In what ways am I currently leading my home well?
- Where have I been neglectful in leadership?
- What practical step can I take this week to reflect Christ's leadership more clearly?

WEEK 2

Honouring Your Wife

"Likewise, you husbands, dwell with them with understanding, giving honour to the wife, as to the weaker vessel, and as being heirs together of the grace of life, that your prayers may not be hindered."

1 PETER 3:7 (NKJV)

Observation

Peter exhorts husbands to honour their wives as fellow heirs of God's grace. To honour is not optional — it is commanded. Dishonour not only wounds a wife but also obstructs a husband's prayers.

Interpretation

To honour your wife is to esteem, value, and treat her with dignity as God's precious daughter. It means recognising her as an equal partner in grace, not diminishing her role. Dishonour dishonours God, while honour magnifies Him within the marriage covenant.

Illustration

Imagine a priceless piece of fine china. It is not handled carelessly but treasured, guarded, and treated with respect. In the same way, a wife is not to be taken for granted but cherished as a gift from God of immeasurable worth.

Correlation

- **Ephesians 5:33** — Husbands must love their wives.
- **John 4:7–26** — Jesus honours the Samaritan woman with dignity and truth.
- **Proverbs 31:28** — A godly wife is praised by her husband.

Application

- Speak words of genuine appreciation daily.
- Show respect for your wife in public and in private.
- Respond attentively to her emotional needs.
- Serve her practically as an act of love and honour.

Prayer

Gracious Father, thank You for the precious gift of my wife. Forgive me where I have failed to honour her as I should. Teach me to treasure her in my thoughts, words, and actions. May my love for her reflect Christ's love for the Church, and may our marriage bring glory to You. Amen.

Journalling Prompts

- *Do I consistently honour my wife in word and deed?*
- *Where have I failed to show her proper esteem?*
- *What deliberate act of honour will I practise this week?*

WEEK 3

Loving as Christ Loves

*"Husbands, love your wives,
just as Christ also loved the church
and gave Himself for her."*

EPHESIANS 5:25 (NKJV)

OBSERVATION

Paul calls husbands to mirror the love of Christ — a love defined by sacrifice, faithfulness, and total commitment.

INTERPRETATION

Christ's love for the Church was neither conditional nor self-serving. It was selfless, enduring, and sacrificial — even to the point of death. A husband is called to reflect this same quality of love towards his wife.

ILLUSTRATION

Consider a firefighter who risks his life to save others. His act is not motivated by comfort or convenience but by sacrifice. In the same way, a husband demonstrates true love when he chooses his wife's wellbeing above his own desires.

Correlation

- **John 15:13** — Greater love has no one than this: to lay down one's life.
- **Colossians 3:19** — Husbands are commanded to love their wives.
- **1 John 3:16** — By this we know love, because Christ laid down His life for us.

Application

- Surrender a personal preference for the sake of your wife's good.
- Practise patience and kindness, especially under pressure.
- Serve her in small but meaningful ways.
- Pray daily with and for her, inviting God's love to flow through you.

Prayer

Lord Jesus, teach me to love my wife as You love the Church — with sacrifice, patience, and devotion. Free me from selfishness and help me to reflect Your unfailing love in every word and deed. May my marriage become a living picture of Your grace. Amen.

Journalling Prompts

- *How does my love currently reflect Christ's love?*
- *What hinders me from showing unconditional love?*
- *What specific sacrifice can I make this week to strengthen our marriage?*

WEEK

Working in Unity With Your Wife

*"For this reason a man shall leave his father
and mother and be joined to his wife,
and the two shall become one flesh."*

EPHESIANS 5:31 (NKJV)

OBSERVATION

Marriage is a covenant of oneness — spiritually, emotionally, and physically.

INTERPRETATION

Unity in marriage does not mean uniformity. It is about harmony, shared vision, and mutual commitment. Division weakens a marriage, but unity strengthens it.

ILLUSTRATION

Picture two rowers in a boat. If they pull in different directions, the boat turns in circles. When they row in rhythm, they move forward with strength. Marriage works the same way — progress depends on unity.

Correlation

- **Amos 3:3** — Can two walk together unless they are agreed?
- **Matthew 19:6** — What God has joined together, let no one separate.
- **Ecclesiastes 4:9–10** — Two are better than one.

Application

- Listen carefully before making decisions.
- Pray together before taking action.
- Resolve disagreements quickly and with humility.
- Affirm your wife as your God-given partner.

Prayer

Father, thank You for joining me and my wife as one. Help me to pursue unity with her in heart and purpose. Teach me to listen, forgive quickly, and lead with humility. May our oneness be a testimony of Your love. Amen.

Journalling Prompts

- *Where are we walking in unity?*
- *Where do disagreements most often arise?*
- *What practical step can I take this week to strengthen our oneness?*

WEEK 5

Fatherhood as Responsibility, Not Just Childbearing

"I write to you, fathers, because you have known Him who is from the beginning."

1 JOHN 2:13 (NKJV)

OBSERVATION

John addresses fathers not for their biological role, but for their spiritual maturity and relationship with God.

INTERPRETATION

True fatherhood is stewardship. Any man can father children, but a godly father nurtures them in the fear of the Lord and leaves a legacy of faith.

ILLUSTRATION

A gardener does not stop at planting seeds. He waters, prunes, shields, and tends them until they mature into fruitful trees. Likewise, a father invests consistently in the growth of his children.

CORRELATION

- **Proverbs 22:6** — Train up a child in the way he should go.
- **1 Corinthians 4:15** — A father imparts care and guidance.
- **Hebrews 12:6** — God disciplines those He loves.

APPLICATION

- Spend intentional, undistracted time with your children.
- Pray for them by name.
- Model Christlike behaviour consistently.
- Teach them one truth from Scripture each week.

PRAYER

Heavenly Father, thank You for entrusting me with children. Help me to nurture and guide them in Your ways. May I reflect Your love and discipline, and leave them a legacy of faith that endures. Amen.

JOURNALLING PROMPTS

- *Do I see fatherhood as a responsibility or merely a title?*
- *What legacy am I building for my children?*
- *What step can I take this week to be a more intentional father?*

WEEK 6

Companionship in Marriage

"Two are better than one, because they have a good reward for their labour. For if they fall, one will lift up his companion."

ECCLESIASTES 4:9-10 (NKJV)

OBSERVATION

God designed marriage as a partnership of companionship. The husband and wife are called to walk together — supporting, encouraging, and strengthening one another.

INTERPRETATION

Companionship in marriage is more than sharing space or responsibilities. It is the bond of friendship, communication, and mutual care. A husband must be present — emotionally, mentally, and spiritually — to his wife.

ILLUSTRATION

Think of two mountain climbers roped together. Each depends on the other for safety and progress. When one slips, the other steadies the line. In marriage, companionship means holding one another up through every climb, storm, and season.

Correlation

- **Genesis 2:18** — It is not good that man should be alone.
- **Malachi 2:14** — Your wife is your companion and the wife of your covenant.
- **1 Thessalonians 5:11** — Encourage one another and build each other up.

Application

- Spend quality time together without distractions.
- Listen with empathy, not impatience.
- Share your goals, fears, and hopes openly.
- Be your wife's closest friend and confidant.

Prayer

Lord, thank You for the gift of companionship in marriage. Help me to be a faithful friend and partner to my wife. Teach me to listen with understanding, speak with grace, and love with patience. May our companionship reflect the unity of Your Spirit. Amen.

Journalling Prompts

- *How strong is our companionship at present?*
- *What activities strengthen our bond the most?*
- *How can I become more emotionally available to my wife this week?*

WEEK 7

Communication That Builds Connection

"Let your speech always be with grace, seasoned with salt, that you may know how you ought to answer each one."

COLOSSIANS 4:6 (NKJV)

Observation

Words have the power to build or to break. The quality of communication between a husband and wife determines the depth of their connection.

Interpretation

Healthy communication is not just about speaking — it is about listening, understanding, and responding with love. Many marital challenges stem from miscommunication, assumptions, or silence. A wise husband guards his tongue, listens attentively, and speaks to heal, not to hurt.

Illustration

A bridge connects two sides separated by water. Strong communication builds that bridge daily. Neglect it, and the connection weakens; nurture it, and the relationship thrives.

Correlation

- **Proverbs 18:21** — Death and life are in the power of the tongue.
- **James 1:19** — Be swift to hear, slow to speak, slow to anger.
- **Ephesians 4:29** — Let no corrupt word proceed out of your mouth.

Application

- Practise active listening — focus fully when your wife speaks.
- Choose your words prayerfully, not impulsively.
- Avoid sarcasm, criticism, or dismissive tones.
- Speak encouragement and affirmation every day.

Prayer

Father, help me to speak words that build, heal, and strengthen my marriage. Teach me to listen with patience and respond with grace. May my words draw my wife closer to You and to me. Amen.

Journalling Prompts

- *How well do I listen when my wife speaks?*
- *What words or attitudes have hurt our communication?*
- *What can I say or do this week to rebuild deeper connection?*

WEEK 8

Faithfulness in All Things

"Moreover it is required in stewards that one be found faithful."
1 CORINTHIANS 4:2 (NKJV)

OBSERVATION

Faithfulness is one of the most essential virtues of a godly husband. It reflects integrity, loyalty, and consistency in thought, word, and action.

INTERPRETATION

To be faithful means to be dependable — in love, character, and responsibility. Faithfulness is not limited to marital fidelity; it extends to one's spiritual life, stewardship, and integrity. God calls every husband to mirror His unwavering faithfulness within the home.

ILLUSTRATION

A lighthouse stands firm through storms and darkness, guiding ships to safety. Its light does not flicker with the wind. Likewise, a faithful husband remains steady through trials, guiding his family with constant love and unwavering devotion.

CORRELATION

- **Proverbs 20:6** — A faithful man, who can find?
- **Lamentations 3:22–23** — Great is Your faithfulness.
- **Matthew 25:21** — Well done, good and faithful servant.

APPLICATION

- Keep your promises, both small and large.
- Be honest and transparent in all your dealings.
- Stay consistent in prayer and devotion with your wife.
- Guard your heart and mind from unfaithful thoughts or actions.

PRAYER

Faithful God, thank You for Your steadfast love and reliability. Help me to reflect Your faithfulness in every area of my life. Strengthen me to be loyal, honest, and consistent in my marriage, my words, and my walk with You. Amen.

JOURNALLING PROMPTS

- *Am I faithful in every aspect of my marriage?*
- *Where have I been inconsistent or careless?*
- *What step can I take today to demonstrate faithfulness to God and my wife?*

WEEK 9

The Husband as Priest of the Home

*"You also, as living stones, are being built up
a spiritual house, a holy priesthood,
to offer up spiritual sacrifices acceptable
to God through Jesus Christ."*

1 PETER 2:5 (NKJV)

OBSERVATION

Every believer is called into a royal priesthood, but within marriage, the husband carries a specific responsibility — to lead his home in worship, prayer, and spiritual covering.

INTERPRETATION

As priest, a husband stands between God and his family, interceding on their behalf and guiding them toward godliness. His role is not about authority but about spiritual responsibility. When he leads in prayer, devotion, and moral integrity, he becomes a channel through which God's grace flows into the home.

ILLUSTRATION

In the Old Testament, the priest entered the temple to offer sacrifices for the people. Today, a husband serves as a living priest — not by presenting burnt offerings, but by presenting his life, words, and leadership as daily sacrifices pleasing to God.

Correlation

- **Job 1:5** — Job offered sacrifices for his family continually.
- **Joshua 24:15** — As for me and my house, we will serve the Lord.
- **Hebrews 4:16** — Let us come boldly to the throne of grace.

Application

- Lead family prayers and devotions regularly.
- Pray for your wife and children by name.
- Model holiness in speech, thought, and conduct.
- Create an atmosphere in your home that honours God's presence.

Prayer

Heavenly Father, thank You for entrusting me with the priestly role within my home. Teach me to intercede faithfully, to lead spiritually, and to serve with humility. Let my home be filled with Your presence, peace, and power. Amen.

Journalling Prompts

- *How consistent am I in leading my home spiritually?*
- *What changes can I make to strengthen our family's devotion?*
- *How can I better reflect the priestly heart of Christ in my home?*

WEEK 10

The Husband as Prophet of the Home

*"Surely the Lord God does nothing,
unless He reveals His secret
to His servants the prophets."*

AMOS 3:7 (NKJV)

OBSERVATION

A prophet is one who hears from God and speaks His truth faithfully. In the context of marriage, the husband is called to listen to God and declare His Word over his home.

INTERPRETATION

As prophet, a husband becomes God's mouthpiece within the family — guiding, instructing, and speaking life according to Scripture. This role requires spiritual sensitivity and a heart tuned to God's voice. Without revelation, a home lacks direction. A husband who prays, listens, and speaks the truth in love establishes divine order and protection.

ILLUSTRATION

Just as a lighthouse warns ships of unseen dangers, a prophetic husband provides vision and guidance for his family. He discerns the spiritual climate of his home and speaks words that align his household with God's purpose.

Correlation

- **Genesis 18:17–19** — God reveals His plans to Abraham, who instructs his household.
- **Proverbs 29:18** — Where there is no vision, the people perish.
- **Ephesians 5:26** — The husband sanctifies his wife through the Word.

Application

- Spend time in God's Word daily to discern His will.
- Speak blessings and Scripture over your family.
- Share what God lays on your heart with humility and wisdom.
- Guard your words — let them always align with truth and grace.

Prayer

Lord, open my ears to hear Your voice clearly. Help me to lead my family by speaking Your truth with love and conviction. May every word I declare bring encouragement, direction, and peace to my home. Amen.

Journalling Prompts

- *How often do I seek God's guidance before making family decisions?*
- *Do my words bring life, encouragement, and direction to my home?*
- *What Scripture can I declare over my family this week?*

WEEK

The Husband as King of the Home

*"The king's heart is in the hand of the Lord,
like the rivers of water;
He turns it wherever He wishes."*

PROVERBS 21:1 (NKJV)

OBSERVATION

A king governs his kingdom with authority and accountability. In the home, the husband's kingship is not about domination but about stewardship, justice, and wise leadership under God's direction.

INTERPRETATION

To be a king in the home means ruling with righteousness, wisdom, and love. A husband governs by example — protecting his family, providing direction, and ensuring peace. His authority must always reflect submission to God's supreme rule. True kingship begins with humility before the King of kings.

ILLUSTRATION

A good king ensures the wellbeing of his people, maintaining order and peace. When he listens to wise counsel and rules with fairness, his kingdom flourishes. Likewise, a husband who governs his home through prayer, patience, and discernment creates an atmosphere where love and harmony thrive.

CORRELATION

- **1 Kings 3:9–12** — Solomon asks for wisdom to govern God's people.
- **Ephesians 5:23** — The husband is the head of the wife, as Christ is the head of the Church.
- **Psalm 72:1–4** — A righteous king brings justice and peace.

APPLICATION

- Lead your home with wisdom, not pride.
- Make decisions prayerfully and justly.
- Protect your family from emotional and spiritual harm.
- Seek counsel from God's Word before taking action.

PRAYER

Sovereign Lord, thank You for entrusting me with leadership in my home. Grant me the wisdom, patience, and humility to govern well. May my leadership reflect Your justice, my heart reflect Your love, and my actions reveal Your grace. Amen.

JOURNALLING PROMPTS

- *How do I currently lead and protect my home?*
- *What does righteous leadership look like in my family?*
- *In what areas do I need God's wisdom to lead more effectively?*

WEEK 12

Spiritual Covering and Paint Protection

"But the Lord is faithful, who will establish you and guard you from the evil one."

2 THESSALONIANS 3:3 (NKJV)

Observation

God protects His people through His faithfulness and power. In the same way, a husband provides spiritual covering and protection for his home through prayer, discernment, and godly leadership.

Interpretation

To be a spiritual covering means to stand in prayer and vigilance over your family. It involves shielding your wife and children from spiritual attacks, harmful influences, and emotional harm. A husband who prays and walks closely with God becomes a conduit of divine protection for his household.

Illustration

A shepherd guards his sheep, staying alert to danger. His presence gives them confidence and peace. Likewise, a husband's spiritual vigilance reassures his family that they are safe under his care and God's covering.

Correlation

- **Job 1:10** — God's hedge of protection around Job and his household.
- **Psalm 91:1–2** — He who dwells in the secret place of the Most High.
- **Ephesians 6:10–11** — Put on the whole armour of God.

Application

- Pray daily for God's protection over your home.
- Be discerning about the influences entering your household.
- Cover your wife and children with Scripture and intercession.
- Maintain purity and integrity — your holiness strengthens your covering.

Prayer

Faithful Father, thank You for being my shield and protector. Help me to stand firm in prayer for my family and to guard our home from all evil. May Your presence surround us, and may our hearts rest under the safety of Your wings. Amen.

Journalling Prompts

- *How intentional am I about spiritually covering my family?*
- *What areas of our home need stronger prayer protection?*
- *What daily habit can I adopt to strengthen my spiritual vigilance?*

W E E K

Financial Stewardship in Marriage

"Moreover it is required in stewards that one be found faithful."
1 CORINTHIANS 4:2 (NKJV)

OBSERVATION

God calls every believer to be a faithful steward of the resources entrusted to them. In marriage, financial stewardship reflects trust, unity, and responsibility before God.

INTERPRETATION

Money can either strengthen or strain a marriage. Wise stewardship begins with recognising that all resources belong to God. The husband, as head of the home, must lead by example — practising generosity, discipline, and accountability. Financial harmony flows from shared goals, transparent communication, and dependence on God's wisdom.

ILLUSTRATION

A farmer who manages his field diligently ensures future harvests. He sows wisely, plans carefully, and guards against waste. Likewise, financial stewardship in marriage requires prudence, patience, and faith — investing in what glorifies God and blesses the family.

Correlation

- **Proverbs 21:5** — The plans of the diligent lead surely to plenty.
- **Luke 16:10–11** — Faithfulness in little leads to faithfulness in much.
- **Malachi 3:10** — Bring all the tithes into the storehouse.

Application

- Pray before making financial decisions.
- Be transparent with your wife about income and expenses.
- Establish a family budget and honour it.
- Give generously and prioritise God's kingdom.

Prayer

Father, thank You for every blessing and resource You have placed in my care. Help me to manage finances with integrity and wisdom. Teach me to lead my family in faith, generosity, and contentment, that our home may honour You in all things. Amen.

Journalling Prompts

- *How do I currently demonstrate faithfulness in financial stewardship?*
- *Are there areas where I need to be more transparent or disciplined?*
- *How can I involve my wife in our financial planning this week?*

WEEK 14

Building a Home on Prayer

*"Unless the Lord builds the house,
they labour in vain who build it."*

PSALM 127:1 (NKJV)

Observation

Every lasting home is built not merely on effort, but on prayer. Prayer invites God's presence, establishes peace, and aligns the family with His purpose.

Interpretation

A praying husband builds a praying home. Prayer strengthens the foundation of marriage, shapes decisions, and sustains unity. When communication with God is consistent, the family's spiritual structure stands firm — even through trials.

Illustration

A house built on sand may look beautiful, but it cannot endure storms. Only the home founded on Christ — through prayer and obedience — remains standing. A husband who leads in prayer builds spiritual walls that protect his family from collapse.

Correlation

- **Matthew 7:24–25** — The wise man builds his house on the rock.
- **Philippians 4:6–7** — In everything by prayer and supplication.
- **James 5:16** — The effective, fervent prayer of a righteous man avails much.

Application

- Establish daily prayer time with your wife or family.
- Keep a family prayer journal to record God's faithfulness.
- Begin and end your day with thanksgiving.
- Make prayer your first response, not your last resort.

Prayer

Lord, teach me to build my home on the firm foundation of prayer. May Your presence fill every room, every decision, and every moment of our family life. Let our home be known as a house of prayer where Your peace reigns. Amen.

Journalling Prompts

- *How consistent is our family prayer life?*
- *What obstacles often hinder us from praying together?*
- *What one change can I make this week to strengthen prayer in our home?*

WEEK

Leading by Example

*"In everything set them an example
by doing what is good. In your teaching
show integrity, seriousness and soundness
of speech that cannot be condemned."*

TITUS 2:7-8 (NIV)

OBSERVATION

Leadership in the home is most effective when modelled through example. Words instruct, but actions inspire.

INTERPRETATION

A husband's example sets the spiritual and moral tone of the household. His faithfulness, integrity, and consistency become a living message to his wife and children. When a husband lives what he teaches, his influence endures. True leadership is not declared — it is demonstrated.

ILLUSTRATION

A lamp does not argue with darkness; it simply shines. Likewise, a husband who walks in righteousness naturally illuminates the path for those who follow. His quiet consistency often speaks louder than his most persuasive words.

Correlation

- **1 Timothy 4:12** — Be an example in word, conduct, love, spirit, faith, and purity.
- **Philippians 3:17** — Follow my example, as I follow Christ.
- **Matthew 5:16** — Let your light shine before others.

Application

- Examine your conduct — would you follow your own example?
- Practise integrity in every decision and action.
- Let your words and behaviour align with your faith.
- Lead your family by demonstrating humility, love, and self-control.

Prayer

Lord, help me to lead by example in every area of my life. Let my words be truthful, my actions honourable, and my heart steadfast before You. May my life inspire faith and obedience in my family, and may Christ be seen through me. Amen.

Journalling Prompts

- *What example am I currently setting for my family?*
- *Do my actions consistently reflect my beliefs?*
- *What area of my life most needs alignment with God's Word?*

WEEK

The Power of Humility in Marriage

*"Humble yourselves, therefore,
under God's mighty hand,
that He may lift you up in due time."*

1 PETER 5:6 (NIV)

Observation

Humility is strength under control — the ability to submit to God's will and to serve others with grace. In marriage, humility is the key that opens the door to peace, understanding, and lasting unity.

Interpretation

A humble husband does not insist on his own way but seeks harmony and truth. Pride breeds conflict, but humility invites God's favour. When a man humbles himself before God, he gains the grace to love, to forgive, and to lead gently. Humility is not weakness; it is spiritual maturity expressed through meekness.

Illustration

When Jesus washed His disciples' feet, He demonstrated that true greatness is found in serving others. Likewise, when a husband serves his wife with humility, he reflects Christ's love and draws her heart closer to him.

Correlation

- **Philippians 2:3–5** — Value others above yourself; have the mind of Christ.
- **James 4:10** — Humble yourselves before the Lord, and He will lift you up.
- **Matthew 23:11–12** — The greatest among you shall be your servant.

Application

- Choose gentleness over pride in moments of disagreement.
- Be quick to apologise and slow to defend yourself.
- Serve your wife in simple, meaningful ways this week.
- Pray for the grace to lead with humility, not pride.

Prayer

Lord Jesus, You are the perfect example of humility. Teach me to follow Your example in my marriage. Remove pride from my heart, and fill me with gentleness and grace. May humility guide my words, actions, and leadership in our home. Amen.

Journalling Prompts

- *Do I lead with humility or pride?*
- *When was the last time I apologised first?*
- *How can I demonstrate humility to my wife and children this week?*

WEEK 17

The Husband as a Man of Integrity

"The righteous man walks in his integrity; his children are blessed after him."

PROVERBS 20:7 (NKJV)

Observation

Integrity is the foundation of trustworthy leadership. A man of integrity honours God in both public and private life, setting a spiritual example for his family to follow.

Interpretation

Integrity means being whole — the same person in every setting. It is truthfulness without compromise, consistency without hypocrisy. When a husband walks uprightly, he builds confidence in his marriage and security in his children. Integrity cannot be taught by words alone; it is proven by a life lived transparently before God.

Illustration

A bridge built on weak supports eventually collapses, no matter how beautiful it looks on the surface. Integrity is the hidden structure that keeps a man's life strong. Without it, even success becomes fragile; with it, every aspect of life stands firm.

Correlation

- **Psalm 25:21** — Let integrity and uprightness preserve me.
- **Job 2:3** — Job held fast to his integrity even under trial.
- **Titus 2:7–8** — Show integrity, seriousness, and soundness of speech.

Application

- Keep your word even when it costs you.
- Be honest in financial, relational, and spiritual matters.
- Let your private life reflect your public testimony.
- Confess and correct mistakes quickly before God and your family.

Prayer

Heavenly Father, help me to walk in integrity before You and my family. Let truth guide my decisions, purity shape my motives, and righteousness guard my heart. May my life be a faithful reflection of Your character and grace. Amen.

Journalling Prompts

- *In what areas is my integrity most tested?*
- *Do my private actions align with my public words?*
- *How can I strengthen honesty and consistency in my daily life?*

WEEK 18

Forgiveness in Marriage

*"Be kind and compassionate to
one another, forgiving each other,
just as in Christ God forgave you."*

EPHESIANS 4:32 (NIV)

OBSERVATION

Forgiveness is the heartbeat of every healthy marriage. Without it, resentment grows and love fades. God calls every husband to forgive as freely as Christ has forgiven him.

INTERPRETATION

Forgiveness is not weakness but strength. It means releasing the right to retaliate and choosing reconciliation over bitterness. A forgiving husband mirrors Christ's mercy, creating space for healing and peace in the home. Forgiveness does not deny pain; it surrenders it to God, trusting Him to restore what is broken.

ILLUSTRATION

A clogged pipe cannot carry water freely until it is cleared. Unforgiveness blocks the flow of love and prayer in marriage. When a husband forgives, grace begins to flow again — refreshing the relationship with life and hope.

Correlation

- **Matthew 6:14–15** — Forgive others so that your Father may forgive you.
- **Colossians 3:13** — Bear with one another and forgive as the Lord forgave you.
- **Psalm 103:10–12** — God removes our transgressions as far as the east is from the west.

Application

- Let go of past hurts and release them in prayer.
- Choose to forgive quickly, even when you feel justified.
- Apologise sincerely when you are wrong.
- Ask God to help you rebuild trust where pain has lingered.

Prayer

Merciful Father, thank You for the grace of forgiveness. Teach me to forgive my wife as You have forgiven me — freely, fully, and without condition. Heal my heart from offence, and fill our home with peace, understanding, and renewed love. Amen.

Journalling Prompts

- *Is there anything I still need to forgive my wife for?*
- *Do I find it easy or difficult to apologise when I'm wrong?*
- *What practical step can I take this week to restore harmony in my marriage?*

W E E K

Cultivating Patience in Marriage

"Love is patient, love is kind. It does not envy, it does not boast, it is not proud."

1 CORINTHIANS 13:4 (NIV)

OBSERVATION

Patience is one of love's purest expressions. It allows room for growth, healing, and understanding within marriage. Without patience, even strong relationships can be strained by frustration or unmet expectations.

INTERPRETATION

Patience is the ability to respond with grace when things don't go as planned. It means enduring differences without irritation and waiting on God's timing with faith. A patient husband reflects Christ's love — steady, enduring, and full of compassion. Patience nurtures peace and gives love the time it needs to mature.

ILLUSTRATION

A gardener knows that seeds do not sprout overnight. He tends the soil and waits, trusting that growth will come in time. Likewise, patience in marriage allows God to work in both hearts, producing lasting fruit.

Correlation

- **Romans 12:12** — Be patient in affliction, faithful in prayer.
- **Ecclesiastes 7:8** — The patient in spirit is better than the proud in spirit.
- **James 1:4** — Let patience have its perfect work.

Application

- Slow down before reacting in anger or frustration.
- Give your wife the grace to grow and change at her own pace.
- Pray for God's timing rather than forcing your own.
- Celebrate progress, not perfection, in your relationship.

Prayer

Lord, teach me to be patient as You are patient with me. Help me to respond with love when I am tempted to be harsh or demanding. Fill my heart with Your peace and my words with gentleness, that my patience may strengthen our marriage. Amen.

Journalling Prompts

- *In what situations do I struggle most to be patient?*
- *How can I slow down and show more grace this week?*
- *What has God taught me through seasons of waiting in my marriage?*

WEEK 20

Emotional Mastery in Marriage

*"Better a patient person than a warrior,
one with self-control than one who takes a city."*

PROVERBS 16:32 (NIV)

OBSERVATION

Emotions are powerful gifts from God, designed to help us connect, empathise, and respond meaningfully to life. Yet when emotions rule us instead of being ruled by the Spirit, they can damage relationships and hinder peace in the home. God calls every husband to cultivate emotional mastery — to respond, not react.

INTERPRETATION

Emotional mastery is not emotional suppression. It means being aware of one's feelings and submitting them to the control of the Holy Spirit. A husband led by the Spirit learns to manage anger, disappointment, fear, and frustration with wisdom and grace. True strength is not seen in outward dominance, but in the quiet restraint that reflects Christ's peace within.

ILLUSTRATION

A thermostat doesn't react to the temperature around it — it regulates it. Likewise, a husband with emotional mastery sets the tone for his home.

CORRELATION

- **Proverbs 29:11** — A fool vents all his feelings, but a wise man holds them back.
- **James 1:19–20** — Be quick to listen, slow to speak, slow to become angry.
- **Galatians 5:22–23** — The fruit of the Spirit includes self-control.

APPLICATION

- Practise pausing before responding in moments of irritation or conflict.
- Ask the Holy Spirit to help you identify emotional triggers and replace reaction with reflection.
- Choose gentleness in tone, even when correcting or disagreeing.
- Model emotional discipline before your wife and children — let them see grace under pressure.

PRAYER

Heavenly Father, teach me to master my emotions through the power of Your Spirit. When I am tempted to react in anger or impatience, help me to pause and choose wisdom. Fill my heart with peace, my tongue with gentleness, and my home with calm. Amen.

JOURNALLING PROMPTS

- *Which emotions do I struggle most to manage well?*
- *How do my reactions affect the emotional atmosphere of my home?*
- *What specific practice can I adopt this week to respond with wisdom and grace?*

WEEK 21

The Husband as a Peacemaker

*"Blessed are the peacemakers,
for they will be called children of God."*

MATTHEW 5:9 (NIV)

Observation

Peace does not happen by accident; it is cultivated intentionally. God calls husbands to be peacemakers — to guard unity, resolve conflict, and maintain an atmosphere of calm in the home.

Interpretation

Being a peacemaker means taking the initiative to heal divisions rather than fuel them. A husband reflects Christ when he chooses reconciliation over pride and calmness over confrontation. Peace is not merely the absence of conflict but the presence of righteousness and love. A peaceful home becomes a sanctuary where God's Spirit dwells freely.

Illustration

A gardener removes weeds regularly to keep flowers thriving. In the same way, a husband must remove bitterness, harsh words, and resentment to allow love to grow. Peace requires daily care and constant attention.

Correlation

- **Romans 12:18** — If it is possible, live at peace with everyone.
- **Hebrews 12:14** — Pursue peace with all people and holiness.
- **James 3:18** — Peacemakers sow in peace and reap righteousness.

Application

- Be the first to seek resolution in times of disagreement.
- Create an environment of calm communication and respect.
- Avoid harsh or defensive words; choose gentleness instead.
- Pray for wisdom to handle tension with grace and patience.

Prayer

Prince of Peace, thank You for reconciling me to the Father. Help me to carry that same peace into my home. Teach me to respond with gentleness, to speak with grace, and to pursue reconciliation above all else. May Your peace reign in our marriage. Amen.

Journalling Prompts

- *Do I bring peace or tension into my home?*
- *What practical steps can I take to resolve current conflicts?*
- *How can I become more intentional about fostering peace daily?*

WEEK 22

The Power of Faith in Family Life

"Now faith is the substance of things hoped for, the evidence of things not seen."

HEBREWS 11:1 (NKJV)

OBSERVATION

Faith is the foundation of every godly home. It shapes how we see challenges, how we make decisions, and how we respond to God's promises. A husband's faith influences the spiritual climate of his entire family.

INTERPRETATION

Faith is not wishful thinking — it is confident trust in God's Word, even when circumstances appear uncertain. A husband who walks by faith sets an example of dependence on God rather than on his own understanding. His trust builds courage in his wife and security in his children. Faith in action turns ordinary homes into testimonies of God's power and provision.

ILLUSTRATION

When Abraham obeyed God and left his homeland, he did not know where he was going — but his faith shaped generations. Likewise, a husband's faith-filled obedience often becomes the seed of blessings that extend beyond his lifetime.

Correlation

- **2 Corinthians 5:7** — We walk by faith, not by sight.
- **Romans 10:17** — Faith comes by hearing the Word of God.
- **Mark 9:23** — All things are possible to him who believes.

Application

- Demonstrate faith through obedience, even in uncertainty.
- Speak words of belief and encouragement during challenges.
- Involve your family in faith-filled prayer for specific needs.
- Keep a record of answered prayers to build family testimony.

Prayer

Heavenly Father, thank You for the gift of faith. Help me to trust You completely and to lead my family by example. Strengthen our faith to believe for the impossible, and let our home reflect confidence in Your promises. Amen.

Journalling Prompts

- *How does my faith influence my family's outlook on life?*
- *In what area of our family life is God asking me to trust Him more?*
- *What testimony of faith can I share with my wife and children this week?*

WEEK 23

The Husband as a Man of Prayer

"Then he spoke a parable to them, that men always ought to pray and not lose heart."

LUKE 18:1 (NKJV)

Observation

Prayer is the lifeline of a godly man. It is through prayer that a husband connects with God, gains wisdom for leadership, and draws strength to love his family well.

Interpretation

A praying husband builds a praying home. His prayers create spiritual covering, open divine doors, and invite God's presence into every situation. The more a man prays, the more he aligns his will with God's. Prayer is not just a duty — it is a relationship of trust and dependence that shapes everything he does.

Illustration

Just as a pilot maintains constant communication with the control tower to stay on course, a husband must stay connected with God through prayer to navigate family life safely. Without prayer, he risks drifting off course.

Correlation

- **1 Thessalonians 5:17** — Pray without ceasing.
- **James 5:16** — The effective, fervent prayer of a righteous man avails much.
- **Philippians 4:6–7** — Pray about everything with thanksgiving.

Application

- Begin each day in prayer before making decisions.
- Pray with your wife and children regularly.
- Keep a prayer list for family, friends, and needs.
- Thank God for answered prayers to strengthen faith.

Prayer

Lord, make me a man of prayer — faithful, focused, and full of faith. Help me to seek Your presence daily and to depend on You for every decision I make. Let my prayers cover my family and draw Your peace into our home. Amen.

Journalling Prompts

- *How consistent am I in my prayer life?*
- *Do I pray with my wife and children often enough?*
- *What specific prayers will I focus on this week for my family?*

WEEK 24

Walking in the Word

*"Your word is a lamp to my feet
and a light to my path."*

PSALM 119:105 (NKJV)

OBSERVATION

God's Word is both a guide and a foundation. It lights the path ahead, keeping husbands grounded in truth and steady in every season of life and marriage.

INTERPRETATION

To walk in the Word means to live daily by its principles — allowing Scripture to shape thoughts, speech, and decisions. The husband who builds his life on God's Word walks securely, leads wisely, and loves faithfully. Without the Word, direction fades and confusion reigns. With it, clarity, peace, and strength abound.

ILLUSTRATION

A traveller who follows a reliable map never loses his way. In the same way, a husband who follows God's Word avoids pitfalls and finds confidence in every step, knowing he walks according to divine truth.

Correlation

- **Joshua 1:8** — Meditate on the Word day and night for success.
- **James 1:22** — Be doers of the Word, not hearers only.
- **Colossians 3:16** — Let the Word of Christ dwell in you richly.

Application

- Read and meditate on Scripture daily.
- Share the Word with your wife and children each week.
- Memorise key verses that speak to your current season.
- Apply one biblical principle practically in your home this week.

Prayer

Lord, thank You for the light of Your Word. Help me to walk in its truth and lead my family by its wisdom. Let Scripture guide my choices, strengthen my faith, and transform our home into a place where Your Word is honoured. Amen.

Journalling Prompts

- *How often do I turn to God's Word for guidance?*
- *What Scripture is shaping my thoughts and actions this week?*
- *How can I make the Word more central in my family life?*

WEEK 25

The Husband as a Man of Wisdom

"If any of you lacks wisdom, let him ask of God, who gives to all liberally and without reproach, and it will be given to him."

JAMES 1:5 (NKJV)

OBSERVATION

Wisdom is one of the greatest needs in marriage and family life. It is not merely knowledge, but the God-given ability to apply truth rightly in every situation.

INTERPRETATION

A wise husband makes decisions through discernment and prayer. He listens before speaking and seeks God's guidance before acting. Wisdom guards a home from unnecessary conflict and helps a husband lead with balance and understanding. True wisdom begins with humility and reverence for God — it cannot be earned, only received.

ILLUSTRATION

When King Solomon asked for wisdom rather than wealth or power, God was pleased and gave him both understanding and blessing. In the same way, when a husband values wisdom above all else, his home becomes a place of peace, direction, and divine favour.

Correlation

- **Proverbs 2:6** — The Lord gives wisdom; from His mouth come knowledge and understanding.
- **Ecclesiastes 7:12** — Wisdom preserves those who have it.
- **Colossians 1:9–10** — Be filled with the knowledge of His will in all wisdom and understanding.

Application

- Ask God daily for wisdom in your words, actions, and decisions.
- Listen carefully before responding to challenges at home.
- Learn from Scripture, godly counsel, and experience.
- Model humility — wisdom flourishes in a teachable heart.

Prayer

Father, You are the source of all wisdom. Fill me with divine understanding and discernment as I lead my family. Teach me to make decisions that honour You and bring peace to our home. May my life reflect the wisdom that comes from above — pure, gentle, and full of mercy. Amen.

Journalling Prompts

- *In what areas of my life do I need more wisdom right now?*
- *How do I usually respond when I don't understand something?*
- *What step can I take to become a more discerning husband?*

WEEK 26

The Husband as Provider

"But if anyone does not provide for his own, and especially for those of his household, he has denied the faith and is worse than an unbeliever."

1 TIMOTHY 5:8 (NKJV)

OBSERVATION

God calls every husband to be a provider — not only of material needs, but also of emotional stability, spiritual guidance, and love. Provision goes beyond income; it encompasses care, presence, and protection.

INTERPRETATION

A husband's role as provider mirrors God's own nature. The Lord provides for His children out of love and responsibility, and He expects husbands to do likewise. Providing for the home requires diligence, planning, and prayer. Yet it also demands balance — recognising that material provision alone cannot sustain a family without spiritual and emotional nourishment.

ILLUSTRATION

Just as a shepherd ensures his flock has food, safety, and direction, a husband must look after every aspect of his family's wellbeing.

True provision means anticipating needs, meeting them with wisdom, and trusting God for strength when resources are limited.

Correlation

- **Philippians 4:19** — My God shall supply all your need.
- **Proverbs 13:22** — A good man leaves an inheritance to his children's children.
- **Genesis 22:14** — The Lord will provide.

Application

- Take responsibility for the physical, emotional, and spiritual wellbeing of your family.
- Plan and manage resources with wisdom and prayer.
- Trust God as your ultimate source, not your job or income.
- Express gratitude for what you have and model contentment before your family.

Prayer

Jehovah Jireh, my Provider, thank You for meeting all our needs. Help me to provide for my family with diligence, love, and faith. Teach me to trust You as my source and to lead my home with contentment, wisdom, and generosity. Amen.

Journalling Prompts

- *Do I see provision as only financial, or as a whole-life responsibility?*
- *In what ways can I better provide emotionally and spiritually for my family?*
- *How can I model trust in God's provision this week?*

WEEK 27

The Husband as Protector

*"The name of the Lord is a strong tower;
the righteous run to it and are safe."*

PROVERBS 18:10 (NKJV)

OBSERVATION

God has placed within every husband the responsibility to protect — not through fear or control, but through love, prayer, and wisdom. His protection reflects God's own heart as a refuge and defender of His people.

INTERPRETATION

Protection in marriage extends beyond physical safety. A husband protects his family spiritually by covering them in prayer, emotionally by providing security and reassurance, and relationally by maintaining peace and stability. True protection does not dominate or restrict; it nurtures and guards what is precious. A protector leads with courage and discernment, not intimidation.

ILLUSTRATION

Just as a shepherd watches over his flock and keeps alert for danger, a husband must stay spiritually awake — discerning threats to his home and interceding before harm comes. His vigilance, paired with love, creates an environment where his wife and children feel safe and valued.

Correlation

- **Nehemiah 4:14** — Fight for your families, your sons and daughters.
- **Psalm 121:7–8** — The Lord will keep you from all harm.
- **Ephesians 6:13** — Put on the whole Armour of God.

Application

- Pray daily for the protection of your wife and children.
- Be attentive to emotional needs and sources of stress within your home.
- Guard your family from harmful influences — spiritual, moral, and relational.
- Lead with peace, creating a home where love casts out fear.

Prayer

Lord, thank You for being my refuge and protector. Help me to reflect Your care by protecting my family with wisdom, strength, and compassion. Keep my heart sensitive to danger and my spirit steadfast in prayer. May our home be a place of safety, trust, and peace. Amen.

Journalling Prompts

- *How do I currently protect my family — spiritually, emotionally, and physically?*
- *Are there areas where I have neglected to provide covering?*
- *What specific action can I take this week to strengthen protection in our home?*

WEEK 28

The Husband as Encourager

*"Therefore encourage one another
and build each other up,
just as in fact you are doing."*

1 THESSALONIANS 5:11 (NIV)

OBSERVATION

Encouragement is a powerful expression of love. A husband's words and actions can either uplift or crush the spirit of his wife and children. God calls every husband to be an encourager — one who speaks life, hope, and strength into his home.

INTERPRETATION

Encouragement is more than positive talk; it is Spirit-inspired affirmation that reminds others of God's faithfulness. A husband who encourages his wife helps her flourish in confidence and purpose. His steady words of support build emotional security and strengthen the bond of unity in marriage. Just as Christ continually affirms His Church, so should a husband affirm his wife.

ILLUSTRATION

A small spark can ignite a great fire. In the same way, one sincere word of encouragement can rekindle hope and motivation in a weary heart. Encouragement doesn't always require much — just intentional love expressed through kind words and thoughtful actions.

Correlation

- **Proverbs 12:25** — A kind word cheers the heart.
- **Hebrews 3:13** — Encourage one another daily.
- **Ephesians 4:29** — Let your words impart grace to those who hear.

Application

- Speak daily words of affirmation to your wife and children.
- Recognise and celebrate small victories in your home.
- Be present when your family faces challenges — offer reassurance, not criticism.
- Pray that your words will always bring comfort and courage.

Prayer

Heavenly Father, thank You for being my constant encourager. Teach me to speak life, hope, and faith into my family. Let my words build rather than break, and my presence bring strength and peace to those I love. Amen.

Journalling Prompts

- *How often do I intentionally encourage my wife and children?*
- *What negative habits in speech must I replace with uplifting words?*
- *What opportunity can I take this week to speak life into my home?*

WEEK

Restoring Trust After Failure

*"Create in me a clean heart, O God,
and renew a steadfast spirit within me."*

PSALM 51:10 (NKJV)

OBSERVATION

Trust is the foundation of every marriage, yet even the strongest relationships can experience seasons of disappointment or failure.

INTERPRETATION

Restoring trust requires repentance, not excuses. It begins with acknowledging the hurt and taking responsibility for one's actions. True restoration is not about quick fixes; it is about consistency.

ILLUSTRATION

A cracked wall can be repaired, but only when the foundation beneath it is made firm. Likewise, rebuilding trust means addressing the deeper issues beneath the surface.

Correlation

- **Proverbs 28:13** — Whoever conceals their sins does not prosper.
- **James 5:16** — Confess your faults to one another.
- **Colossians 3:9–10** — Do not lie to each other; put on the new self.

Application

- Take ownership of any past failure — admit it without shifting blame.
- Ask your wife for forgiveness sincerely and specifically.
- Be transparent about your actions, intentions, and progress toward change.
- Rebuild trust through consistent truthfulness, reliability, and spiritual accountability.

Prayer

Merciful Father, thank You for Your grace that restores what sin and failure have broken. Create in me a clean heart and renew my integrity. Help me rebuild trust through honesty, humility, and consistency. Amen.

Journalling Prompts

- *Where have I broken trust in my marriage?*
- *What specific actions will I take this week to rebuild reliability and transparency?*
- *How can I invite the Holy Spirit to help me maintain integrity daily?*

W E E K 30

The Husband as Servant Leader

*"Whoever wants to become great among
you must be your servant, and whoever wants to
be first must be your slave—just as the Son of Man
did not come to be served, but to serve,
and to give His life as a ransom for many."*

MATTHEW 20:26-28 (NIV)

Observation

Jesus redefined leadership through service. In God's design, a husband leads not by domination or authority, but through humility, sacrifice, and love.

Interpretation

Servant leadership begins with the heart. A husband who leads like Christ seeks the wellbeing of his family above his own comfort. He listens, guides, and sacrifices to see his wife and children thrive. True authority in the home flows from love, not control. When a husband serves his family with humility, he mirrors the leadership of Christ — strong, compassionate, and selfless.

Illustration

When Jesus washed His disciples' feet, He demonstrated that leadership means service. Likewise, a husband leads best when he is willing to meet needs that may seem small or unseen. His strength is expressed through tenderness, and his leadership through humility.

Correlation

- **Philippians 2:3–5** — Have the same mindset as Christ Jesus, who humbled Himself.
- **Ephesians 5:25** — Husbands, love your wives as Christ loved the Church.
- **John 13:14–15** — I have set you an example that you should do as I have done for you.

Application

- Lead by example through serving your wife and children.
- Value their needs and perspectives above your own convenience.
- Be quick to listen and slow to demand.
- Model humility and grace in every decision.

Prayer

Lord Jesus, thank You for showing me that true leadership is service. Teach me to lead my home with humility, patience, and love. Help me to serve my family as You serve the Church, and may my leadership reflect Your heart in all I do. Amen.

Journalling Prompts

- *How do I currently serve my family?*
- *Do I lead through humility or through control?*
- *What act of service can I perform this week to reflect Christ's example?*

WEEK 31

The Husband as Visionary

"Write the vision and make it plain on tablets,
that he may run who reads it."

HABAKKUK 2:2 (NKJV)

OBSERVATION

Vision gives direction and meaning to life and marriage. A husband without vision leads a home that drifts; a husband with godly vision leads a family that flourishes.

INTERPRETATION

A visionary husband seeks God's purpose for his family and communicates it clearly. He does not live reactively, but intentionally — setting spiritual, emotional, and practical goals that align with God's Word. Vision empowers the family to move together in unity, hope, and purpose. When a husband receives divine direction, he becomes a steward of destiny within his home.

ILLUSTRATION

A ship without a compass is at the mercy of the winds. But when guided by a clear course, it reaches its destination. Likewise, a husband with God's vision provides focus, direction, and courage, even when life's storms arise.

Correlation

- **Proverbs 29:18** — Where there is no vision, the people perish.
- **Joshua 24:15** — As for me and my house, we will serve the Lord.
- **Ephesians 5:15–17** — Be wise and understand what the Lord's will is.

Application

- Seek God's vision for your marriage and family through prayer.
- Write down the goals and values God lays on your heart.
- Share that vision regularly with your wife and children.
- Revisit and realign your plans with God's purpose each season.

Prayer

Lord, give me Your vision for my home. Help me to lead with clarity, purpose, and faith. Open my eyes to see what You desire for our family, and grant me the courage to follow it wholeheartedly. May our home reflect Your will and direction. Amen.

Journalling Prompts

- *What vision do I currently have for my marriage and family?*
- *Have I communicated this vision clearly and consistently?*
- *What step can I take this week to align our home with God's purpose?*

WEEK 32

The Husband as Builder of Legacy

"A good man leaves an inheritance to his children's children, but the wealth of the sinner is stored up for the righteous."

PROVERBS 13:22 (NKJV)

OBSERVATION

Every husband is building a legacy — intentionally or unintentionally. Legacy is not only about material inheritance, but about values, faith, and the godly example that outlives one's lifetime.

INTERPRETATION

A godly legacy begins with daily obedience. What a husband models in his home — integrity, prayer, love, and discipline — becomes the blueprint his children follow. Legacy is built through consistent faithfulness, not grand achievements. The husband who prioritises God's principles today lays foundations for generations to come.

ILLUSTRATION

A wise builder knows that a strong structure requires a solid foundation. In the same way, a husband who builds his family on the truth of God's Word ensures that his descendants stand firm long after he is gone. His influence becomes a lasting testimony of faith.

Correlation

- **Psalm 78:5–7** — Teach your children so that future generations may know God.
- **Deuteronomy 6:6–7** — Impress these commands upon your children.
- **2 Timothy 1:5** — Faith first lived in your grandmother and mother now lives in you.

Application

- Live intentionally with your children and family in mind.
- Invest time, wisdom, and prayer into shaping their faith.
- Leave a legacy of love, faith, and integrity — not just possessions.
- Evaluate regularly: what will my children remember most about me?

Prayer

Heavenly Father, help me to build a legacy that honours You. May my words, choices, and faith inspire generations to follow You wholeheartedly. Teach me to live each day with eternity in mind, building something that will outlast my lifetime. Amen.

Journalling Prompts

- *What kind of legacy am I building in my family right now?*
- *How do my daily actions influence the next generation?*
- *What values do I most want my children and grandchildren to remember?*

WEEK 33

Resolving Conflict God's Way

*"A gentle answer turns away wrath,
but a harsh word stirs up anger."*

PROVERBS 15:1 (NIV)

OBSERVATION

Conflict is inevitable in every marriage. Yet, God's Word does not call husbands to avoid conflict — but to resolve it in a way that honours Him.

INTERPRETATION

Conflict handled in the flesh produces division, but conflict handled in the Spirit produces growth. Winning an argument is not the goal; restoring unity is.

ILLUSTRATION

Two stones in a river may collide, but over time the water smooths their rough edges. Likewise, conflict can refine a marriage when handled with love.

Correlation

- **Ephesians 4:26–27** — Do not let the sun go down while you are still angry.
- **Matthew 5:9** — Blessed are the peacemakers.
- **Colossians 3:13** — Bear with each other and forgive one another.

Application

- Pray before entering any difficult conversation.
- Listen with empathy — seek to understand before responding.
- Replace harsh words with soft answers that bring peace.
- Choose reconciliation over self-justification.

Prayer

Lord Jesus, teach me to resolve conflict in a way that honours You. When emotions rise, help me to respond with gentleness and humility. Guard my words and my tone, and fill my heart with Your peace. Amen.

Journalling Prompts

- *How do I typically respond when conflict arises in my marriage?*
- *What patterns or words tend to make tension worse?*
- *What step can I take this week to practise godly conflict resolution in my home?*

WEEK 34

The Power of Agreement in Marriage

"Again, I say to you that if two of you agree on earth concerning anything that they ask, it will be done for them by My Father in heaven."

MATTHEW 18:19 (NKJV)

OBSERVATION

Agreement is one of the most powerful principles in marriage. When a husband and wife walk in unity — spiritually, emotionally, and practically — their prayers carry multiplied power, and their home experiences divine harmony.

INTERPRETATION

Agreement in marriage is not about uniformity, but unity of purpose. It means aligning hearts and minds under God's will. Disagreement is inevitable, but when handled with grace and humility, it can lead to stronger understanding. A husband who values agreement builds trust, stability, and spiritual strength in his home.

ILLUSTRATION

Two people rowing in the same boat must paddle in the same direction to move forward. If they row in opposite directions, the boat only spins in circles. In the same way, unity between husband and wife ensures progress, while division leads to stagnation.

Correlation

- **Amos 3:3** — Can two walk together unless they are agreed?
- **Ecclesiastes 4:9–10** — Two are better than one; if one falls, the other lifts him up.
- **Philippians 2:2** — Be like-minded, having the same love, being of one accord.

Application

- Seek God together before making major family decisions.
- Discuss issues calmly and prayerfully until peace is reached.
- Avoid pride — choose unity over being "right."
- Affirm your commitment to walk in agreement daily.

Prayer

Father, thank You for the gift of unity in marriage. Teach me to seek peace and agreement with my wife in all things. Help us to align our hearts with Your will so that our prayers may be powerful and our home filled with harmony. Amen.

Journalling Prompts

- *Are there areas where my wife and I struggle to agree?*
- *How can I become more flexible and understanding in our discussions?*
- *What can I do this week to strengthen unity in our marriage?*

W E E K 35

The Husband as Spiritual Leader

"For the husband is the head of the wife as Christ is the head of the church, His body, of which He is the Saviour."

EPHESIANS 5:23 (NIV)

OBSERVATION

Spiritual leadership is one of the husband's highest callings. It is not a position of dominance but of service, responsibility, and example — guiding the family toward a deeper relationship with God.

INTERPRETATION

A spiritual leader sets the tone for the home's relationship with God. He leads through prayer, consistent devotion, and obedience to Scripture. His leadership is seen not in control but in his willingness to follow Christ wholeheartedly. When a husband walks closely with God, his family is strengthened by his faith, steadied by his example, and inspired by his love.

ILLUSTRATION

A lighthouse does not shout at ships — it simply shines. In the same way, a husband leads spiritually not by force, but by example. His steady walk with God becomes a guiding light for his wife and children to follow.

Correlation

- **Joshua 24:15** — As for me and my house, we will serve the Lord.
- **1 Timothy 3:4–5** — He must manage his own household well.
- **Deuteronomy 6:6–7** — Teach God's commandments diligently to your children.

Application

- Take initiative in leading family devotions and prayer.
- Model a lifestyle of worship, integrity, and humility.
- Encourage spiritual growth in your wife and children.
- Seek God's guidance before making key decisions.

Prayer

Lord, thank You for entrusting me with the spiritual leadership of my home. Teach me to lead with love, wisdom, and humility. Help me to set an example of faith that inspires my family to walk closely with You every day. Amen.

Journalling Prompts

- *How consistently do I lead my family in prayer and devotion?*
- *What areas of my spiritual life need strengthening?*
- *What one thing can I do this week to grow as a spiritual leader in my home?*

W E E K 36

The Husband as Intercessor

"I looked for someone among them who would build up the wall and stand before Me in the gap on behalf of the land so I would not destroy it, but I found no one."

EZEKIEL 22:30 (NIV)

OBSERVATION

Intercession is one of the most vital responsibilities of a godly husband. It is the act of standing before God on behalf of his wife, children, and family — bridging the gap through prayer, faith, and compassion.

INTERPRETATION

An intercessor is one who carries the burdens of others to God in prayer. A husband who intercedes for his family demonstrates love in its purest form. His prayers bring divine protection, healing, and breakthrough. When he stands in the gap, he positions his household under God's mercy and favour. Intercession is not optional for the spiritual head of the home — it is essential.

ILLUSTRATION

Moses stood in the gap between God and Israel, pleading for mercy, and the nation was spared. In the same way, when a husband intercedes faithfully, heaven responds. His quiet prayers may never be seen, but their effects will be felt across generations.

Correlation

- **Job 1:5** — Job continually prayed and offered sacrifices for his family.
- **1 Samuel 12:23** — Far be it from me to sin against the Lord by ceasing to pray for you.
- **James 5:16** — The prayer of a righteous man is powerful and effective.

Application

- Set aside regular time to pray specifically for your wife and children.
- Intercede for their spiritual growth, protection, and purpose.
- Keep a prayer journal to track answered prayers and ongoing needs.
- Partner with your wife in prayer for shared burdens and family goals.

Prayer

Father, thank You for the privilege of intercession. Teach me to stand faithfully in prayer for my family. Help me to carry their needs before You with compassion and persistence. Let my prayers release Your power, protection, and peace over our home. Amen.

Journalling Prompts

- *How often do I intercede specifically for each member of my family?*
- *What area of our family life most needs consistent prayer right now?*
- *How can I make intercession a daily habit rather than an occasional act?*

WEEK 37

The Husband as Shepherd of His Home

"I am the good shepherd. The good shepherd gives His life for the sheep."

JOHN 10:11 (NKJV)

OBSERVATION

The image of a shepherd captures the essence of a husband's calling — to lead, guide, protect, and care for his family with love and sacrifice. A shepherd's leadership is gentle but firm, compassionate yet courageous.

INTERPRETATION

As shepherd of the home, a husband's role is to nurture his family spiritually and emotionally. He must know the needs of his wife and children, guide them with wisdom, and defend them against anything that threatens their peace or growth. True shepherding is not about control; it is about loving leadership that reflects Christ's care for His Church.

ILLUSTRATION

A shepherd knows his sheep by name and leads them to safe pastures. When danger approaches, he does not flee — he stands between the flock and the threat. In the same way, a husband must be vigilant in guarding his home, ensuring that love, truth, and godliness flourish within it.

Correlation

- **Psalm 23:1–3** — The Lord is my Shepherd; I shall not want.
- **1 Peter 5:2–3** — Shepherd the flock of God among you, being examples to them.
- **Micah 5:4** — He shall stand and feed His flock in the strength of the Lord.

Application

- Be attentive to the emotional and spiritual wellbeing of your family.
- Lead them by example — through prayer, kindness, and consistency.
- Guard your home against negative influences.
- Be present and available to guide, comfort, and support.

Prayer

Good Shepherd, thank You for leading and protecting me with unfailing love. Help me to reflect Your heart in the way I lead my family. Teach me to guide with wisdom, protect with courage, and care with compassion. Let my home rest securely under Your guidance. Amen.

Journalling Prompts

- *How do I currently shepherd my home — spiritually and emotionally?*
- *What challenges make it difficult for me to lead with gentleness?*
- *How can I reflect the love and care of Christ more effectively this week?*

WEEK 38

The Husband as Teacher of the Word

*"These words that I command you today
shall be in your heart. You shall teach them
diligently to your children, and shall talk of them
when you sit in your house, when you walk by the way,
when you lie down, and when you rise up."*

DEUTERONOMY 6:6-7 (NKJV)

OBSERVATION

A husband is called not only to live by God's Word but also to teach it within his home. His responsibility extends beyond provision and protection — he must also nurture his family's understanding of Scripture.

INTERPRETATION

Teaching the Word begins with example. A husband who studies and applies Scripture naturally influences his family's values, priorities, and faith. His home becomes a place where the Word of God is not only read but lived. Teaching requires consistency, humility, and creativity — bringing truth to life through everyday conversations, actions, and prayer.

ILLUSTRATION

A lamp only lights the room when it is switched on. Similarly, God's Word only illuminates the home when it is spoken, shared, and practised. A husband who teaches the Word ensures that his family walks in light, not darkness.

Correlation

- **Psalm 78:5–7** — Teach your children so that they may put their trust in God.
- **2 Timothy 3:16–17** — All Scripture is inspired by God and useful for teaching.
- **Colossians 3:16** — Let the Word of Christ dwell richly among you.

Application

- Read and discuss Scripture regularly as a family.
- Share biblical lessons during meals, travel, or family devotion time.
- Encourage questions and honest dialogue about God's truth.
- Live what you teach — consistency strengthens credibility.

Prayer

Lord, thank You for entrusting me with the privilege of teaching Your Word in my home. Fill me with wisdom, understanding, and patience. Help me to live out Your truth daily so that my wife and children may grow in faith and love for You. Amen.

Journalling Prompts

- *How consistently do I share God's Word with my family?*
- *What can I do to make our home more centred on Scripture?*
- *How does my example influence how my family values the Word?*

W E E K 39

The Husband as Example of Faith

"Remember your leaders, who spoke the word of God to you. Consider the outcome of their way of life and imitate their faith."

HEBREWS 13:7 (NIV)

OBSERVATION

A husband's faith sets the spiritual tone for the entire home. His example influences how his wife and children trust God, face challenges, and interpret life's struggles.

INTERPRETATION

Faith is both taught and caught. A husband who trusts God in every circumstance becomes a living sermon to his family. When he prays in uncertainty, praises in difficulty, and believes in the face of adversity, his family learns that faith is not a theory but a lifestyle. His calm confidence in God becomes the anchor that steadies the household through every storm.

ILLUSTRATION

When Peter stepped out of the boat to walk on water, the others saw what faith looked like in action. Likewise, when a husband steps out in faith — obeying God even when the outcome is uncertain — his family witnesses the power of trust in motion.

Correlation

- **2 Corinthians 5:7** — We walk by faith, not by sight.
- **Hebrews 11:6** — Without faith it is impossible to please God.
- **Romans 4:20–21** — Abraham did not waver through unbelief but was strengthened in faith.

Application

- Demonstrate faith by trusting God in your decisions and challenges.
- Share testimonies of God's faithfulness with your family.
- Respond to difficulties with prayer rather than worry.
- Encourage your wife and children to believe boldly and expectantly.

Prayer

Lord, help me to be a man of faith whose life inspires trust in You. Strengthen me to stand firm in trials and to lead my family with confidence in Your promises. Let my faith be evident not just in words but in actions that glorify You. Amen.

Journalling Prompts

- *How visible is my faith to my family in daily life?*
- *Do I respond to challenges with fear or with trust in God?*
- *What step of faith is God calling me to take this week?*

WEEK 40

The Husband as Steward of Time

—⚜—

*"See then that you walk circumspectly,
not as fools but as wise, redeeming
the time, because the days are evil."*

EPHESIANS 5:15-16 (NKJV)

OBSERVATION

Time is one of life's most precious resources. How a husband manages his time reflects his priorities and values. God calls husbands to be wise stewards of time — balancing work, rest, family, and devotion.

INTERPRETATION

Every moment is a gift entrusted by God. A wise husband recognises that time wasted cannot be recovered, but time invested in godly pursuits bears eternal fruit. Stewarding time well requires discipline, focus, and intentionality. A husband who manages his time wisely ensures that his family receives not just his provision, but his presence.

ILLUSTRATION

A gardener who tends his plants daily reaps a healthy harvest, but neglect leads to decay. Similarly, when a husband invests time consistently in prayer, family, and growth, his home thrives. Wise time management is not about busyness — it's about purpose.

Correlation

- **Psalm 90:12** — Teach us to number our days, that we may gain a heart of wisdom.
- **Colossians 4:5** — Walk in wisdom toward outsiders, making the best use of time.
- **Ecclesiastes 3:1** — To everything there is a season and a time for every purpose.

Application

- Prioritise daily time with God before all else.
- Schedule quality time with your wife and children regularly.
- Set healthy boundaries between work and family life.
- Reflect weekly on how your time aligns with your values.

Prayer

Lord, thank You for the gift of time. Help me to use it wisely and purposefully. Teach me to prioritise what truly matters — Your will, my family, and my calling. May every hour of my life bring glory to You and blessing to my home. Amen.

Journalling Prompts

- *How do I currently manage my time each day?*
- *What important things have I been neglecting due to busyness?*
- *How can I realign my schedule to honour God and my family more fully?*

WEEK

41

Creating a Culture of Peace at Home

*"Let us therefore make every effort to do
what leads to peace and to mutual edification."*

ROMANS 14:19 (NIV)

OBSERVATION

Peace must be intentionally cultivated. Every husband plays a vital role in shaping the spiritual and emotional atmosphere of his home.

INTERPRETATION

Creating a culture of peace begins in the heart of the husband. True peace is more than the absence of arguments; it is the presence of righteousness, forgiveness, and love.

ILLUSTRATION

A gardener who tends his soil daily keeps weeds from choking the plants. Likewise, a husband who tends to peace regularly removes small irritations before they become major conflicts.

Correlation

- **Psalm 34:14** — Seek peace and pursue it.
- **James 3:18** — Peacemakers who sow in peace reap a harvest of righteousness.
- **Colossians 3:15** — Let the peace of Christ rule in your hearts.

Application

- Begin and end each day with prayer for peace in your home.
- Be intentional about resolving misunderstandings quickly.
- Speak words that heal rather than stir up division.
- Create peaceful family rhythms that invite calm.

Prayer

Father of Peace, help me to be an instrument of peace in my home. Guard my heart from impatience and my tongue from harshness. Let Your peace reign in every conversation and decision. Amen.

Journalling Prompts

- *What attitudes or habits in me disturb the peace at home?*
- *How can I model peace to my wife and children this week?*
- *What new family habit could strengthen calm and unity in our home?*

WEEK 42

The Husband as Anchor in Times of Storm

*"Therefore everyone who hears these words of Mine
and puts them into practice is like a wise man
who built his house on the rock. The rain came down,
the streams rose, and the winds blew and beat
against that house; yet it did not fall,
because it had its foundation on the rock."*

MATTHEW 7:24-25 (NIV)

OBSERVATION

Every family faces storms — seasons of trial, uncertainty, or loss. In such times, the husband's faith and steadiness become the anchor that helps his family remain firm and hopeful.

INTERPRETATION

An anchored husband is one who stands firm on the Word of God. His peace is not shaken by circumstances because his confidence rests in the Lord. His calm presence gives his wife and children security when everything else feels unstable. When he leads with prayer, wisdom, and faith, he becomes a living reminder that God is still in control.

ILLUSTRATION

An anchor keeps a ship from drifting, even when waves are fierce. It doesn't stop the storm, but it prevents the vessel from being swept away. In the same way, a husband grounded in faith holds his family steady, reminding them that God is their refuge.

Correlation

- **Psalm 46:1–2** — God is our refuge and strength, a very present help in trouble.
- **Isaiah 26:3** — You will keep in perfect peace those whose minds are stayed on You.
- **Hebrews 6:19** — This hope we have as an anchor of the soul, firm and secure.

Application

- Respond with calm and faith when challenges arise.
- Lead your family in prayer during difficult times.
- Speak God's promises over your home to build confidence and hope.
- Stay rooted in Scripture — your strength will steady your household.

Prayer

Lord, thank You for being my solid rock and foundation. Help me to remain steadfast in faith so that I may anchor my family through every storm. Let my trust in You bring peace, courage, and confidence to those You've entrusted to my care. Amen.

Journalling Prompts

- *How do I typically respond when life's storms arise?*
- *Do my words and actions bring calm or anxiety to my home?*
- *What Scripture can I stand on to strengthen my faith in times of trial?*

W E E K 43

The Husband as Source of Joy

*"A cheerful heart is good medicine,
but a crushed spirit dries up the bones."*
PROVERBS 17:22 (NIV)

OBSERVATION

Joy is a spiritual strength that sustains relationships and lifts the atmosphere of the home. A husband who cultivates joy becomes a channel of hope and positivity for his family.

INTERPRETATION

True joy is not dependent on circumstances but springs from a heart anchored in God. A joyful husband brings light into his home, creating an environment of laughter, gratitude, and encouragement. His outlook shapes the emotional tone of his family. When he chooses joy even in hardship, he teaches his wife and children to trust God in every season.

ILLUSTRATION

Just as sunlight brings warmth and life to everything it touches, a joyful spirit brightens the entire household. A husband's cheerful presence can turn weariness into strength and frustration into gratitude. Joy, when shared, multiplies.

Correlation

- **Nehemiah 8:10** — The joy of the Lord is your strength.
- **Philippians 4:4** — Rejoice in the Lord always.
- **John 15:11** — My joy may be in you, and that your joy may be full.

Application

- Express gratitude daily, even in small things.
- Create moments of laughter and light-heartedness with your family.
- Replace complaints with words of thanksgiving.
- Let your joy in the Lord be visible — it will strengthen those around you.

Prayer

Father, thank You for the joy that comes from Your presence. Help me to carry that joy into my home every day. Let my words and actions uplift those I love and bring light wherever there is heaviness. May my life reflect Your joy and strength. Amen.

Journalling Prompts

- *How does my attitude affect the emotional tone of my home?*
- *Do I intentionally cultivate joy and gratitude each day?*
- *What can I do this week to bring joy to my wife and children?*

W E E K

The Husband as Spiritual Warrior

"For the weapons of our warfare are not carnal but mighty in God for pulling down strongholds."
2 CORINTHIANS 10:4 (NKJV)

OBSERVATION

Every husband is called to stand as a spiritual warrior — vigilant, prayerful, and ready to defend his home against the enemy's attacks. Spiritual warfare is not fought with physical weapons but with faith, prayer, and the Word of God.

INTERPRETATION

A husband who understands his role as a warrior realises that his battle is not against people but against spiritual forces that seek to divide and destroy. He fights on his knees, interceding for his wife, children, and home. Through prayer, fasting, and obedience, he takes authority over fear, confusion, and temptation. His strength lies not in aggression but in steadfast faith and spiritual discernment.

ILLUSTRATION

A watchman on the wall stays alert through the night, guarding against unseen danger. Likewise, a husband must remain spiritually awake — discerning when to pray, when to speak, and when to stand still in faith. His vigilance protects his home from unseen harm.

Correlation

- **Ephesians 6:10–11** — Put on the whole armour of God to stand against the devil's schemes.
- **1 Peter 5:8–9** — Be alert; resist the enemy, standing firm in faith.
- **James 4:7** — Submit to God, resist the devil, and he will flee from you.

Application

- Start each day by putting on the spiritual armour of God.
- Pray strategically over your home, marriage, and family.
- Stand firm against spiritual compromise or temptation.
- Declare God's promises when fear or doubt arise.

Prayer

Mighty God, thank You for equipping me to fight spiritual battles. Teach me to stand firm in faith and to guard my home through prayer. Clothe me with Your armour, fill me with discernment, and let Your power prevail in every area of my family's life. Amen.

Journalling Prompts

- *How alert am I to the spiritual battles affecting my home?*
- *What practical steps can I take to strengthen my spiritual defence?*
- *Which promise of God will I declare over my family this week?*

WEEK 45

The Husband as Vessel of Grace

"Husbands, in the same way be considerate as you live with your wives, and treat them with respect as the weaker partner and as heirs with you of the gracious gift of life, so that nothing will hinder your prayers."

1 PETER 3:7 (NIV)

OBSERVATION

Grace is the divine influence that transforms hearts and relationships. A husband who becomes a vessel of grace reflects Christ's kindness, patience, and compassion in his home.

INTERPRETATION

To be a vessel of grace means to embody gentleness and understanding, even when circumstances are difficult. A godly husband extends forgiveness quickly, listens patiently, and corrects lovingly. His actions and words reveal the same grace that he himself has received from God. When a husband leads with grace, his marriage becomes a reflection of God's unconditional love.

ILLUSTRATION

A clay vessel carries water to refresh others, though it may not be perfect itself. Likewise, a husband filled with God's grace refreshes his family — not because he is flawless, but because he allows God's Spirit to flow through him freely.

Correlation

- **Colossians 4:6** — Let your conversation always be full of grace.
- **Ephesians 4:32** — Be kind and compassionate, forgiving one another.
- **John 1:16** — From His fullness we have all received grace upon grace.

Application

- Respond with grace rather than anger or criticism.
- Speak kindly and build up your wife and children.
- Be patient with weaknesses — in others and in yourself.
- Remember that your grace towards your family reflects your walk with God.

Prayer

Lord, fill me with Your grace so that I may pour it into my marriage and family. Teach me to be gentle, patient, and understanding. Let my words and actions reflect the love and mercy I have received from You. Amen.

Journalling Prompts

- *How do I demonstrate grace in my marriage and home?*
- *Are there areas where I struggle to be patient or understanding?*
- *How can I better reflect God's grace to my wife and children this week?*

WEEK 46

The Husband as Example of Love

*"Husbands, love your wives,
just as Christ loved the church
and gave Himself up for her."*
EPHESIANS 5:25 (NIV)

OBSERVATION

Love is the foundation of true leadership in marriage. A husband's love, modelled after Christ's sacrificial example, becomes the clearest reflection of God's heart within the home.

INTERPRETATION

To love as Christ loves means to give selflessly, forgive freely, and serve humbly. It is not based on feelings or circumstances but on commitment and grace. A husband's love should bring security, nurture, and strength to his wife and family. When he loves well, his home becomes a sanctuary of peace and belonging.

ILLUSTRATION

A candle gives light by burning itself. Similarly, true love often costs something — time, pride, comfort, or convenience. Yet it is through such sacrifice that a husband's love mirrors the heart of Christ and brings warmth to his household.

Correlation

- **1 Corinthians 13:4–7** — Love is patient, love is kind; it never fails.
- **1 John 4:19** — We love because He first loved us.
- **John 15:12–13** — Love one another as I have loved you; greater love has no one than this.

Application

- Show love through daily acts of kindness and attentiveness.
- Forgive quickly and refuse to hold grudges.
- Express affection in both words and actions.
- Pray for a heart that loves your wife as Christ loves the Church.

Prayer

Lord Jesus, thank You for showing me perfect love through Your sacrifice. Help me to love my wife selflessly and unconditionally. Teach me to demonstrate love through patience, compassion, and grace so that my marriage reflects Your divine love. Amen.

Journalling Prompts

- *How does my love for my wife reflect Christ's example?*
- *In what ways can I show deeper love and understanding this week?*
- *What attitudes or habits hinder me from expressing love freely?*

WEEK

The Husband as Encourager of Faith

*"Let us hold unswervingly to the hope
we profess, for He who promised is faithful.
And let us consider how we may spur
one another on toward love and good deeds."*

HEBREWS 10:23-24 (NIV)

OBSERVATION

A husband's role includes encouraging faith — in his wife, his children, and himself. His words and example should strengthen their confidence in God and remind them of His faithfulness.

INTERPRETATION

Faith grows stronger when nurtured by encouragement. A husband who continually points his family to God during challenges builds spiritual resilience in their hearts. His faith-filled outlook turns fear into hope and discouragement into determination. When he chooses to see through the eyes of faith, he lifts his entire household.

ILLUSTRATION

When Joshua faced the daunting task of leading Israel, God repeatedly told him, "Be strong and courageous." In the same way, a husband encourages his family to stand firm and trust God, even when life's circumstances seem uncertain. His words become a lifeline that fuels their faith.

Correlation

- **Romans 10:17** — Faith comes by hearing, and hearing by the Word of God.
- **1 Thessalonians 5:11** — Encourage one another and build each other up.
- **Psalm 31:24** — Be strong, and let your heart take courage, all you who hope in the Lord.

Application

- Speak words that remind your family of God's promises.
- Pray together when challenges arise rather than worrying.
- Share testimonies of answered prayers to strengthen faith.
- Be an example of perseverance and trust in every circumstance.

Prayer

Heavenly Father, help me to be an encourager of faith in my home. Let my words and actions point my family to You. Strengthen me to stand firm in belief and to inspire others to do the same. May our home be filled with confidence in Your unfailing love and faithfulness. Amen.

Journalling Prompts

- *How do I currently encourage faith in my family?*
- *Do my words reflect faith or fear during challenges?*
- *What can I do this week to help my wife and children grow stronger in faith?*

W E E K 48

Guarding the Gates of Your Home

*"Above all else, guard your heart,
for everything you do flows from it."*

PROVERBS 4:23 (NIV)

OBSERVATION

Every home has gates — entry points that allow influences to enter the hearts and minds of its members.

INTERPRETATION

Guarding your home is not about control but about stewardship. A godly husband recognises that influences shape thoughts and faith.

ILLUSTRATION

A city with open gates is vulnerable to attack, but one with strong, guarded walls stands secure. Likewise, discernment keeps a home safe.

Correlation

- **Nehemiah 4:14** — Fight for your families.
- **Psalm 101:3** — I will set before my eyes no vile thing.
- **Ephesians 6:11** — Put on the full armour of God.

Application

- Evaluate media, music, and conversation influences.
- Set clear moral boundaries rooted in love.
- Replace harmful influences with uplifting ones.
- Pray daily for discernment and grace.

Prayer

Lord, make me a faithful guardian of my home. Help me to discern what honours You and remove anything that grieves Your Spirit. Fill our hearts with peace and truth. Amen.

Journalling Prompts

- *What gates in my home need greater spiritual vigilance?*
- *Are there influences I've allowed that diminish peace or purity?*
- *What step can I take this week to strengthen our spiritual covering?*

WEEK 49

The Husband as Peacemaker and Mediator

*"Blessed are the peacemakers,
for they will be called children of God."*
MATTHEW 5:9 (NIV)

OBSERVATION

Peace within the home does not happen by chance; it is cultivated by those who intentionally pursue it. As head of the family, the husband carries the responsibility to mediate, reconcile, and maintain harmony when tension arises.

INTERPRETATION

A peacemaker does not avoid conflict — he addresses it with grace, truth, and humility. A husband as mediator listens to both sides, seeks understanding, and responds with fairness. His aim is not to win arguments but to restore relationships. When he brings calm instead of chaos and healing instead of hurt, he reflects the nature of Christ, the ultimate Mediator between God and man.

ILLUSTRATION

Just as a bridge connects two separated sides, a peacemaker connects hearts divided by misunderstanding. His patience and wisdom make reconciliation possible, turning moments of conflict into opportunities for growth.

Correlation

- **Romans 12:18** — If it is possible, as far as it depends on you, live at peace with everyone.
- **James 3:17–18** — Wisdom from above is peace-loving, gentle, and full of mercy.
- **2 Corinthians 5:18** — God has given us the ministry of reconciliation.

Application

- Be quick to listen and slow to speak in moments of disagreement.
- When tension arises, pray before reacting.
- Seek to understand rather than to prove your point.
- Lead your home with patience, gentleness, and fairness.

Prayer

Lord, make me a vessel of peace in my home.
Teach me to handle conflict with wisdom and humility.
Help me to bring reconciliation where there is division
and calm where there is unrest. Let Your peace reign
in our hearts and in our home. Amen.

Journalling Prompts

- *How do I typically handle conflict within my family?*
- *What changes can I make to become more of a peacemaker?*
- *Is there a relationship in my home or family that needs healing right now?*

WEEK 50

The Husband as Source of Strength and Stability

"Be on your guard; stand firm in the faith; be courageous; be strong."

1 CORINTHIANS 16:13 (NIV)

OBSERVATION

A husband's strength provides stability for his family. When he stands firm in faith and conviction, his home becomes secure — not because he controls it, but because he anchors it in God's truth and presence.

INTERPRETATION

Strength in marriage is more than physical endurance; it is spiritual resilience and emotional steadiness. A husband demonstrates true strength when he faces adversity with faith, makes decisions with wisdom, and supports his wife and children with consistency. His presence calms storms, his words build courage, and his actions inspire trust. Stability flows from his unwavering dependence on God.

ILLUSTRATION

A tree with deep roots stands unmoved by the wind. In the same way, a husband rooted in God's Word remains firm despite life's pressures. His confidence in the Lord keeps his family grounded, even in seasons of uncertainty.

Correlation

- **Isaiah 40:31** — Those who wait on the Lord shall renew their strength.
- **Psalm 62:6** — He alone is my rock and my salvation; I shall not be shaken.
- **Ephesians 6:10** — Be strong in the Lord and in His mighty power.

Application

- Draw daily strength from prayer and God's Word.
- Be emotionally present and dependable for your family.
- Handle challenges with calm faith, not fear or anger.
- Encourage your family to find their strength in God.

Prayer

Lord, make me a pillar of strength and stability in my home. Help me to rely on Your power, not my own. Let my faith and peace bring security to my wife and children, and may our family stand firm together through every season of life. Amen.

Journalling Prompts

- *How do I demonstrate strength and stability in my home?*
- *What areas of my life need deeper roots in God's Word?*
- *How can I help my family stand firm in faith during challenging times?*

W E E K 51

The Husband as Instrument of Blessing

*"The righteous man walks in his integrity;
his children are blessed after him."*
PROVERBS 20:7 (NKJV)

OBSERVATION

A godly husband is not only blessed by God — he becomes a conduit of blessing to his wife, children, and generations to come. His obedience, integrity, and prayers create a spiritual covering that brings favour upon his household.

INTERPRETATION

When a husband walks uprightly before God, his life becomes a channel through which divine blessings flow. His decisions shape the destiny of his family, and his faith invites God's favour into their home. Being an instrument of blessing requires intentional living — choosing righteousness, walking in humility, and maintaining a thankful heart. Through his words, actions, and intercession, a husband releases life and grace into his family.

ILLUSTRATION

Just as a river nourishes everything along its banks, a husband who abides in God continually refreshes his home. His presence brings encouragement, his prayers invite protection, and his generosity strengthens those around him.

Correlation

- **Genesis 12:2** — I will bless you, and you shall be a blessing.
- **Psalm 112:1–2** — Blessed is the man who fears the Lord; his descendants will be mighty.
- **Numbers 6:24–26** — The Lord bless you and keep you; the Lord make His face shine upon you.

Application

- Live with integrity and humility before God and your family.
- Speak words of blessing over your wife and children daily.
- Give generously of your time, resources, and love.
- Remember that your obedience to God blesses generations after you.

Prayer

Lord, thank You for making me an instrument of Your blessing. Help me to walk in integrity and to live in a way that honours You. Let my life bring joy, peace, and favour to my family and all who know me. May Your blessings overflow through me to generations to come. Amen.

Journalling Prompts

- *In what ways do I currently bring blessing to my family?*
- *How can I use my words and actions to encourage and uplift those around me?*
- *What legacy of blessing do I want to leave behind?*

W E E K 52

Living as a Lifelong Priest

"Through Jesus, therefore, let us continually offer to God a sacrifice of praise—the fruit of lips that openly profess His name."

HEBREWS 13:15 (NIV)

OBSERVATION

The husband's priestly role is not temporary but lifelong. God invites every husband to represent Him in the home.

INTERPRETATION

To live as a lifelong priest means making your life an altar to God. A priestly husband models holiness, humility, and dependence on God.

ILLUSTRATION

Priests in the Old Testament kept the fire on the altar burning continually. Today, a husband keeps his spiritual fire alive through prayer and devotion.

Correlation

- **Joshua 24:15** — As for me and my house, we will serve the Lord.
- **1 Peter 2:9** — You are a royal priesthood.
- **Romans 12:1** — Present your bodies as a living sacrifice.

Application

- Make prayer and worship a daily habit.
- Intercede for your family and future generations.
- Model holiness and devotion.
- Keep your spiritual fire burning through Scripture and gratitude.

Prayer

Heavenly Father, thank You for the privilege of serving as priest in my home. Let my life be an altar of worship and my actions a reflection of Your holiness. Amen.

Journalling Prompts

- *How have I grown in my priestly role?*
- *What daily practices will I continue to keep the spiritual fire alive?*
- *What legacy of faith do I want my family to remember?*

Closing Reflection

As you complete this 52-week journey, pause to reflect on the path you have walked. Each devotion has invited you to grow as a husband — stronger in faith, deeper in love, and more Christlike in character.

This devotional is not about perfection but about progress — small, faithful steps of obedience that build a marriage rooted in Christ. The lessons here are not meant to end but to continue as rhythms of life. Revisit the Scriptures, prayers, and journalling prompts often. Let them remind you of your sacred calling as a husband.

Remember

- Love is a daily choice, not a one-time vow.
- Prayer is a constant covering, not an occasional ritual.
- Growth is a lifelong journey, not a quick destination.

Your marriage is a gift entrusted to you by God. As you continue beyond these weeks, may you embrace that calling with humility, joy, and courage. May your love reflect Christ's love more fully each day — a living testimony of His grace.

Prayer of Commitment

Lord, thank You for leading me through this devotional journey. Strengthen me to walk daily in love, humility, and faith. May my marriage reflect Your glory, and may my life be a blessing to my wife, my family, and generations to come. Amen.

Final Journalling Prompts

- *What is the greatest lesson I've learnt through this journey?*
- *How has my love for my wife grown over these weeks?*
- *What commitments will I carry forward into the next season of our marriage?*

OTHER BOOKS
BY THE AUTHOR

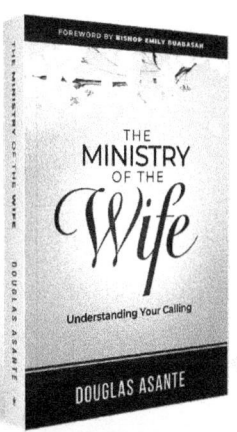
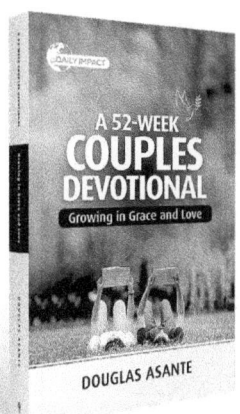

AVAILABLE ON
amazon   amazon kindle

---

www.dasante.org.uk

www.ingramcontent.com/pod-product-compliance
Lightning Source LLC
Chambersburg PA
CBHW021014090426
42738CB00007B/786